Late Self-Portraits

Late Self-Portraits

POEMS BY **MARY MORRIS**

WHEELBARROW BOOKS ▪ *East Lansing, Michigan*

♾ The paper used in this publication meets the minimum requirements of ANSI/NISO Z39.48-1992 (R 1997) (Permanence of Paper).

 Wheelbarrow Books
Michigan State University Press
East Lansing, Michigan 48823-5245

Library of Congress Control Number: 2021937289

ISBN 978-1-61186-422-9 (paper)
ISBN 978-1-60917-689-1 (PDF)
ISBN 978-1-62895-455-5 (ePub)
ISBN 978-1-62896-449-3 (Kindle)

Cover design by Erin Kirk
Cover photo by *Red Turban*, by Daniëlle van Zadelhoff

Visit Michigan State University Press at *www.msupress.org*

With the publication of Mary Morris's collection of poems, *Late Self-Portraits*, the Residential College in the Arts and Humanities (RCAH) Center for Poetry at Michigan State University offers its ninth book in our Wheelbarrow Books Poetry Series. Clearly, we pay homage to William Carlos Williams and his iconic poem, "The Red Wheelbarrow." Readers will remember the poem begins "so much depends upon . . . " that red wheelbarrow.

For many of us, so much depends upon the wonderful collections of poetry we can find to help us in times of crisis. As we find ourselves in 2021, a year into the COVID-19 global pandemic with over 521,000 deaths in this country alone, it is a comfort that Mary Morris gives us a book of poems where grief, loss, and death present themselves in the personages of historical figures, artists, family, and self, many of whom suffer from illness, but who are determined to love and survive. "Is the body sanctuary or battle?" Morris asks in "Portrait of Orpheus, Frida Kahlo, Love & Death." After an epileptic seizure, the poet finds herself "Between breath and death   fading voices of ghosts. / Someone murmurs   *She's lost her color.*" Death is never very far away, the author knows, and the stories she tells, both historic and personal, are engaging and powerful, rich with image and detail. The pacing of poems in *Late Self-Portraits* alternates between longer more narrative poems and shorter more simplistic ones, small breaths we need to take, before we can go on to the next portrait, or tale.

Portrait of an Old Dog with Crooked Teeth
Faithful shadow, jigsaw
fence of crooked teeth.
All night bark. Protector.
Sheath.

The spiritual component of many of Morris's poems, often understated but apparent, should give readers of this collection solace and hope. She is adept at weaving together strands of religion, history, the natural world, and feminism in the portraits she draws and can place them all into a personal space. In "Winter Chapel," she concludes

Watching birds dart from branch
to branch in order to keep warm,
I make fliers about women's rights

to circulate in wind, notice that the patio's
circular table, sparkled diamond-white,
resembles a marriage cake.

This is the night to bundle up,
place candles and leaves
in the table's center, light them,

recite vows of hope and peace
to a country gone awry, in ceremony
for this wedding of winter while

standing in a spotlight of flames
within a dark cold, planning
revolution.

Morris is a poet skilled in her ability to use language, who understands the power of sound and image, the juxtaposing of dark and light, the personal and the historic. Sometimes there is despair; sometimes there is humor as in "Portrait of Notre-Dame with my Son" where her son goes into a confessional, intrigued by the little booths, though he is not Catholic:

Forty minutes later, my son walks up to me.
I told him I am unconcerned about the seven
deadly sins. Except for sloth. I don't want to be sloth.

Who among us cannot think of our own *sloth* when we read this, or which of the other seven deadly sins we may have committed? Or fear?

Though these lines appear in the opening poem of *Late Self-Portraits*, "Missing," they are the ones that stay with me throughout the entire collection, even after I have turned the last page. In a time when so many of us have lost those we love to COVID, to cancer, to aging, or the unpredictable, I wish for these lines to hold true: "Occasionally in dreams we receive / a postcard with an unknown stamp / from a place so remote there is no dirt." It's those postcards we watch for, hope for, wait for. Perhaps, in their own way, these poems are those postcards.

As our number of Wheelbarrow Books publications increase, we hope that our audience increases also. Help us spread the word. In the beginning was the word, and the word became the poem. So much depends upon the collaboration of reader, writer, and poem, the intimate ways we come to know one another. So much depends upon this long-term relationship.

—ANITA SKEEN, *Wheelbarrow Books Series Editor*

"*Is the body sanctuary or battle?*" "*Girls with seizures*"; *Late Self-Portraits* is a riveting look into the lives—and bodies—of those suffering from illness. The speaker shapeshifts, taking on the personas of various women throughout history—Joan of Arc, Frida Kahlo, Marie Curie—as well as famous men (Francis Bacon, Dylan Thomas, Jorge Luis Borges). These poems voyage to vibrant, distant places in time and geography, melding past and present. A son wanders the historic streets of Paris at night, and by day enters a cathedral's contemporary glass confessional. A dying mother is a Madonna lighting a cigarette and checking Facebook. A man with HIV bench presses in a "modern Colosseum" among men whose bodies are chiseled like stone. I am moved by the clarity of vision and the tenderness of touch in these poems. This is a speaker who looks closely and renders the seen and unseen masterfully, her gaze lingering on an image just long enough for us to see it, too. When the speaker turns her attention inward, what is revealed is a devastating portrait of illness, a body wracked by seizures. Sanctuary or battle, this body insists on being attended to—raucous with ghosts, horses, pain. These poems sizzle with energy and urgency. I could not look away.

—Leila Chatti

for Daniel, John, and Ken

I thought that I was vanishing, but instead I was only coming true.

—CLIVE JAMES

CONTENTS

I.

II.

Late Self-Portraits

I.

Missing

Saw my brother in a wolf, in wildflowers,
climate change, bobcats, javelina, and praying
mantis, lilac scent, laughter. Saw him howling

himself back onto the sidewalk of his life
before he lay his body in front of a bus, drunk.
I don't know what risk is really, to be
that bare, that happy with ruin.

The dead won't give their secrets away.
Occasionally in dreams we receive
a postcard with an unknown stamp
from a place so remote there is no dirt.

Or bees. No grass. Only air and water.
A blue postcard of a boat unmoored
or single oar afloat. On the back, a message
so faint, or a palimpsest, layer upon
layer upon, illegible.

On anniversaries of their departures
they blow kisses in wind from behind
mountains or sing in disguise through
gale or bird. Then silence. Waif thin.

Let the twilight come. Dusk. Its darker
bright, its mission with night hawk, wolves,
and great horned owls, its ancient fables

in constellations. Letters to the evening
of missing brothers, children, husbands
gone north, and our own two parents
with their creation stories, us.

Gods of a Grand Mal

They come

cause grave   electrical disturbances   in the brain.
I resist   resign   pass out   head to floor   forget
all the names   and places   I knew before.

Between breath and death fading voices of ghosts.
Someone murmurs   *She's lost her color.*

Body robbers—

Trust us   they say *Don't belong   Come   with us.*
And I hear that song   repeated at times   when a witness   to cruelty.

Gods who emit acrid vapors   auras identical to dictators.
A gray silk breath   rises into sky.

I am breathing again   and the gold light of dawn
thrums through my fallen body.

From the floor I hear my son singing from his crib.
His voice inspires   flowers in new life. A want to live.

My family calls me   superstitious   yet surely the ghost still arrives
Δ Δ Δ Δ Δ

from some unknown   residence   place of obscurity
remote sighs.

With faint images   like underdeveloped film
an assimilation   appears   behind windows
whispers itself into curtains.

Salem, America, 1692

Girls with seizures
swallow potions.

Mint cures cramps.
Pennyroyal, menses

to expel the mistake
of a life less cruel.

In 1692, the country
confirmed us possessed—

to be burned at the stake,
sentenced to death.

If we were witches,
they would have known.

We would have hexed
their puritanical bodies,

thrown them into the sea,
drowned them

with their holy scripture,
testaments of murder.

Epileptic

Within the body—
a ghost

Ground   unfastened
Contradicted space

As if falling from a horse
in constant defeat

Day to dark
motion slowed

Nightmare stoked
with trees on fire

Scent of ember   spark
and brain shimmer

Morning body
of all-night snow

The world dusted white
The floor   hard   cold

Appointment with Dr. Siegel

Across the neurosurgeon's massive desk
sits a small pot with a brain cactus.

Maybe it's not funny. I pretend I don't see it.
He speaks of a ten-hour surgery

as if it storms today, yet tomorrow
we set sail for sunny Grenada.

Sometimes tools resemble weapons.
So I departed that office within

a concrete steel obelisk of a medical spire
in the boom-box of Spanish Harlem

where I met the A train, left with the decision
of whether to be blinded and paralyzed

by an operation that would obliterate
the malformation—or take my chances.

I was a new mother.
My blouse flowered with milk.

Intensive Care

In the dream, so deeply subterranean
there are prehistoric fish and serpents.

Above, boats and boards
in the shapes of doors and coffins.

The current, you are either with
or against it.

Study of a Woman in the Woods

Oak   Beech   Kudzu   Harriet
Tubman   child in shackles

Battered by your master
you suffer   head wounds

causing seizure   Epilepsy
Fever dreamer   Secret agent

Activist   suffragist   unlocking
chains   gate keeper

Why did they not anoint *you*
as martyr   my heroine

I hereby declare you saint
majestic   visionary

I call thee hope   sustenance
armor   *curandera*   mirror

You   in the cotton   magnolia
swamp   the come-to

consciousness
trailing the grand mal

Leading the people
from the broken promised land

O Mother   O Moses
Guiding them   Past

the sinners singing gospel
Fleeing   O

Sometimes We Slip Out of Our Bodies

& snow falls through late night poems
The doctor calls the scents I intuit *auras*—

smoke and alcohol aroma
notes of mushroom in a forest

through neurons in the corpus callosum
Sometimes we slip—alerts   a fragrance

before rooms fade and consciousness
wanes   A seizure cripples

bends wind   sparks fire in the brain
A grand mal grows hooves and mane

as earth disappears underneath   losing
ground   forcing the body down

Neurons misfire
Muscles stiffen

Years disappear   morph
through synesthesia

We sing the body warm and cool
Epileptic   Passed out   Stir

on dirt of a foreign universe

Apnea

Chorus of his small body at night.
Bronchial windpipe.

Loud beginning, abrupt ending
of each breath.

Are these the angels of death
floating untimely, stealing rest?

His body is not a building,
house, monument, church.

It is children under shelter waiting
for the rain to end so they can roust

and play, eyes so dark and weary.
A little hymn of him, humming

a song of fight. Restless, his breathing
through such great heights.

Portrait of Joan of Arc (1412–1431)

Steel-clanked in armor, soldiers
mount their steeds, yet it is a girl
who leads the French army to victory.

An epileptic peasant given visions
through archangels. An equestrian teen
dressed like a man with shorn hair.

Charged with heresy—she hears voices
as if possessed and is suspected
of magic and witchcraft.

A warrior afflicted with seizures
is tied to a stake, forced
to watch her horse torched
before she herself is burned alive.

Singe of her innocence.
Char of a tormenter's ungodliness.
Martyred. Our Lady of Resistance
aflame for our world.

Canonization of Joan of Arc, May 1920

Let it be said:

Centuries on, a new king
declares Joan innocent, a martyr .

Beatified, deigned *blessed*
inside Notre-Dame. Canonized.
Most revered Maid of Orleans

enters Sainthood as 30,000 citizens
grasp candles through the evening.

Gasp before extinguishing
flames in the Seine.

French troops will carry her image
into battle, parade banners in air,

wear engraved silver medals
next to their chests.

"I had a daughter born in lawful wedlock who grew up amid the fields and pastures. I had her baptized and confirmed and brought her up in the fear of God. I taught her respect for the traditions of the Church as much as I was able to do given her age and simplicity of her condition. I succeeded so well that she spent much of her time in church and after having gone to confession she received the sacrament of the Eucharist every month. Because the people suffered so much, she had a great compassion for them in her heart and despite her youth she would fast and pray for them with great devotion and fervor. She never thought, spoke, or did anything against the faith. Certain enemies had her arraigned in a religious trial. Despite her disclaimers and appeals, both tacit and expressed, and without any help given to her defense, she was put through a perfidious, violent, iniquitous, and sinful trial. The judges condemned her falsely, damnably and criminally, and put her to death in a cruel manner by fire. For the damnation of their souls and in notorious, infamous, and irreparable loss to me, Isabelle, and mine . . . I demand that her name be restored."

—from ISABELLE, *the mother of Joan of Arc*

Portrait of Marie Laveau

Because the air is a stew
of angel tongue and devil tail

root-buckled   magnolia scent
she purifies the sick   feeds the poor

deciphers her people's epistles
to the Madonna of the diaspora

fashions little bag of gris-gris
necklace from magnet   fingernail

and fish hook   because *she* is the oracle
seamstress of effigies—tapping in bones

sewing in lyrics   A sax player burns
a horn   delivers delirium heat

She sees the future   a king with a dream
Knows   in the underworld of grief

people write with a wishbone given by the Madam
of St. Ann Street   because she listens

to yearning   this queen of aspiration
a princess noir   a woman with answers

People in New Orleans say *Leave*
pound cake at her tomb   Saint Expedite
will carry the sentiment

Vex the political gargoyles in the kingdom
and the glory of shade and gamblers

Roll the dice   utter her name   fuse the heads
of saints to the vertebrae of scientists

while she charms the sun from the darkness
like a newborn rooting for milk—the blessing

all people were meant for   to survive on this island
this crescent above   holy water   Algiers   America

Marie Curie

From Poland to Paris

For a woman of that country
to be educated in physics
she must travel to the Sorbonne

transform a lab in order
to study an unknown
swarm of isotopes

In a laboratory with flasks
and glass beakers for separation
of radium   to a battleground of soldiers

wounded   she and her daughter
trudge the first mobile X-ray
machine through front lines

Aura   Halo   Bone

A surgeon will see through the body
in battlefield for the first time

Radium   Overexposure   a heated chill—
invasive medicine   For what cured
could kill

In another kind of war   the ghost
that haunted   slept in her
blood   ate her bones

* * *

Today at the clinic   I think of her
Madame Curie   as I hold the hand
of a friend   hairless in a hospital bed

following a precise dose of radiation
Aura   Halo   We sense bone
down to marrow

Portrait of Orpheus, Frida Kahlo, Love & Death

In the accident, an entire century swam by—
X-rays, surgeries, resurrections.

Algunas palabras, the few words of encouragement.
Faith—the great exorcist. Healings, failed,
failed again, a haunting.

Frida and Diego move next door to the old hotel
of revolutionaries—their cause.

But how do you fall in love with a man
who is *al fin de todo*, the end of everything?

How do you love a sister who sleeps with your husband
in the middle of October when the air is so still

and full of poetry, the simple-minded condemned
to a lack of mystery?

Some believe the body is an empire filled with past lives
lotería chiquita, small lottery of the living.

Is the body sanctuary or battle? How would one know
in the hospital of paint and knives?

Here, in this *plaza, canciones* spill music of *mi amor*,
drummers beat rhythms like cicadas, guitarists strum
wooden instruments with strings of gut and gold.

I dance with a man named Orpheus whose steps
divert our departure from this *vida breve*, inflicting
thorns in nectar of summer, this dervish of breathing.

Then at once, not.

Tell Me All Your Secrets

of honey and wind.

I will tuck them in—to my vertebrae
one by one.

C-4   the devastation you haul
of your mother

who tried to kill you both
before you were born.

C-6, the lover you couldn't keep.

We never voted on this.
Never trusted the overslight.

I share your memories in my body
like an organ. I seize.

I weep at your discomfort, friend.

Portrait of Caravaggio Painting Death of the Virgin

If he fished the drowned prostitute from the Tiber,
it was so he could pose her as the Madonna

on an empty field of canvas. Love. Mary of
they took my body to be a room for the lord.

She *is* the lord. Flesh, *not flesh.*

From a jar of umber paint, apostles gather grief
over the virtuous, bloated vessel. Magdalena

sits close, face in hands, as the immaculate
soul ascends. What could have been said

between two women who loved the same man?
Caravaggio hears a great requiem—

the calling of *Ave Marias* chorused in his brushes
as he abandons Rome, enters Ephesus.

New Religion

Remove the bloody icons
from your walls.

Wrap them in white gauze.
Perform a decent burial.

Chant gospel,
play Nina Simone.

Pay for a poor woman's abortion.
Make the sign of the swan.

Lay yourself in the sun
like a temple on the mountain.

Be sworn.
Be sworn in.

Winter Chapel

Today I stay home as it snows
and I wonder, how can something so fast
and beautiful be this quiet?

Watching birds dart from branch
to branch in order to keep warm,
I make fliers about women's rights

to circulate in wind, notice that the patio's
circular table, sparkled diamond-white,
resembles a marriage cake.

This is the night to bundle up,
place candles and leaves
in the table's center, light them,

recite vows of hope and peace
to a country gone awry, in ceremony
for this wedding of winter while

standing in a spotlight of flames
within a dark cold, planning
revolution.

Donations, Saint-Sulpice

For two euros
you can light a candle
in the cathedral
of Saint-Sulpice.

Or you can hand it
to the homeless man
hiding in the sacristy

next to the shoes
he has just removed
rain-soaked, one sole gone.

We ran in to escape
the downpour, to listen
to the concert with pipe
organ. Verdi's *Requiem*.

Seven hours until our flight
back home. Two days past
the march of the Parisians'
latest *Résistance*.

If all holy buildings
could shelter
those they exclude,

estates of worship
nearly empty, would house
the homeless, destitute.

Portrait of Notre-Dame with My Son

We cross the Seine to *Île de la Cité*
where sparrows squabble and fountains
murmur, until we find her, Our Lady of Paris.

Twelfth-century gothic. Medieval precipice
of saints. Gargoyles perched along cliffs
of stone. Sinister protectors in the overhang

of history. We make humble our spines,
climb the 387 slender steps
to the belfry with aerial view.

Scope of an ancient forest, Sacré-Cœur,
conversations with statues of winged demons
and celestial beings before our descent.

A return to the nave, in front of a pyramid
of red votives, I light a candle, dark
as the organs of animals, for my family,
friends, the burning planet.

My son asks what is the purpose
of the glass rooms with doors. *The new
confessionals*, I say. *Transparency.*

What do you do in there?
You tell your sins.
I want to do that.
You have to be Catholic.

I'm going anyway.

He takes his place in line outside
the compartments. When his turn, he enters
the windowed room, takes a seat, proceeds
with his first confession to a priest.

I roam the sacristy, view the reliquary,
Crown of Thorns, splinters of the True
Cross, and a Holy Nail that crucified Him.

I check my watch for the third time, walk by the boxes
of sin and forgiveness, repentance, and dark memory.
Son and priest lean across a desk, face each other
animated in conversation. Nowhere near a conclusion.

I circle, visit the fourteen Stations
of the Cross, ponder the painting of Veronica,
who wipes the face of Jesus before his death.

Forty minutes later, my son walks up to me.
*I told him I am unconcerned about the seven
deadly sins. Except for sloth. I don't want to be sloth.*

We walk outside in the cool air, toll of bells
and birdsong, converse over catacombs
on the way home, weave our way through *Place
Saint-Sulpice*, Academia de la Sorbonne.

I don't think you have to worry about it,
I tell him, a dyslexic boy who was bullied
for not reading until fifteen, who carries
volumes in his head on theory and philosophy.

We stop by a café where he tells me, *This
is where Sartre wrote.* A young woman nods
to him and he back to her. Surely, someone
he met last night while I was sleeping

and he was seeing Paris as a young man.

Testament

If I were called in
to assemble a religion

I would construct
all the bones of my dead
into a Colosseum

step inside the center
of that amphitheater

lie down as defeated
gladiator, feed new fires

within, as it appears to be
a cold winter coming on.

And I would conjure
shadow back to body

fill the void of empty
spaces that circulate

under the covers
inside my head.

If You Believe the Seizures Moved On

Hexed. Vanished. Spent

because they have not haunted
in years.   Don't be fooled.

There is a stallion in your shadow
trailing you. See it

galloping on the ridge above
gold-streaked cliffs, spooking

you and the red-tailed hawk,
bull snake, horned toad. Watch

how scaled and feathered creatures
flee. Lie down on earth, mica, stone.

Feel the ground tremble.
Distance and time—

all we can measure. Like a bruise
appearing out of nowhere.

Matadora

In the ring, savvy with composure,
wearing crimson cape and pink
satin trousers.

Assured and vulnerable as any fighter.
Swift, spontaneous, you know
how to ride this.

Let the *picadores* precede death.
You are in dirt, defending
your freedom

up against the bull. Aggressor.
Horns. Strategic, composed,
dancing with the beast.

You are scratched.

It bleeds.

Portrait of Spain, Cubism

A fence of teeth   shifts   slightly in the jaw

in a land where vendors and grocers
entertain the idea of becoming
matadores or *picadores*

from an overabundance   of the shiny blood of oil in a painting by
    El Greco

Background of dark planets	tenebrous shadows on torn velvet
the way Picasso paints her face	shaping the shift of squares
Too much running of the bulls	stampede of sharp planes
So much filigree of gold	trembling in the house of belief
as tiny red harlequins serve	the Mass of Thieves
A litany of perspective	storms of hair and teeth

Guernica—causing even the best of sailors to turn back
toward the land of their mothers and farming

Soft and cooing   doves   the magician's crow   draw us
toward first light—all angles   through stained-glass windows

The Last Castrato

Waking from a dream, in a pensione near the winged lion, down the street
from *Accademia di Musica*, I hear these canaries, voices so velvet I imagine
they are the last castrati. In Venice, gold-leafed baroque, blue damask,
crimson decadence, pre-adolescent sons were sold by poor families
for their voices.

Dolce voce.

Gondolas ferry cargo. Each little boy with the solo of a cherub—shred
of the ethereal world—sluice, severance before vocal cords deepen
into a man. Treble clefs for choirboys, men whose contralto hovered
over the Palace of the Doges, as water murmured under the Bridge
of Sighs. Larynx altered, soprano sweetened.

Morire.

Shiver the evil by a father or mother who received a sack of coins
for sacrificing their young son, I leave this place of beauty and sin,
arrive home across continents, listen to a recording of the last castrato,
an angel in limbo, in pain and splendor between heaven and hell,
so sweet yet vulnerable, singing *Deo.*

In Excelsis Deo.

Prayer Flags

The clinic again—another procedure.
Imagine this time you don't have a body.

Conjure yourself invisible. The image
they capture is the soul

a hundred shades of blue, that you see
its reflection, its affects

and defects. Its impermanent, indelible
mark on whom you have interceded with.

Side effects of the medication—brain traffic,
prayer flags, a green stone in my side

like an introspective eye.

Ars Poetica

I didn't know   the day would be

a set of green stairs

that I would be climbing outside

of my body.

Last Tango in Red

When death makes its move
close enough to dance
breathing down my neck
I want to tango
fall into its arms
in love with the music
swing low
trust its compass
let go
my breath.

II.

Rembrandt, Late Self-Portrait

Crimson, with broken blood vessels,

he forfeits the mirror, eating pears

with a glass of time, listens to snow

fall behind memory, while cadmium

corpuscle, boneblack shadow

and lead white glisten of drooling lip

tell us

how to draw death close,

paint ravens in.

Our Lady of Broken Waters

I walk to the house of my mother
who wears delicate plum skin.

We watch robins feed at her window
as rainwater flows down the *canales*.

I brew her coffee as she lights a cigarette,
checks Facebook. Strolls her walker

to an open drawer, hands me a scarf
to wear on my head.

It looks like a hijab, very pretty,
she whispers. We kiss.

I walk home, observe first snow
on the mountains, an aperture of winter,

and wonder how it will be without
these visitations, after her tumor

has consumed her. My Madonna
of milk, sovereign of the house

lights left on, and her open door.

Fentanyl

Every third day
one of us must replace
the fentanyl patches
on our mother's body.
Her hundred goodbyes,
birds at the windowsill.
Children lift and circle
around her like spirits.
A drug so powerful
placed anywhere
on skin, it will travel
directly to the brain.
Just the correct amount.
Too much and she is overdosed—
fifty times more potent
than morphine. An opioid
so strong, we must sterilize
our hands, dispose gingerly
its envelope. This powerful
transdermal, wild animal
in its formula.
Imbroglio of pain
while the tumor expands.
And the children, angels
circling above
her body again.

Portrait of Borges with His Mother

> *To fall in love is to create a religion that has a fallible god.*
>
> —JORGE LUIS BORGES

Take communion—a lozenge, stone, song,
coin of the body, a dying man.

When Borges becomes blind, his mother wraps him
in her Uruguayan coat, listens as he dictates his mind's
rhythm of images, verses, then scribbles her son's poems.

Under a tree, bees swarm, air warm with aroma
of ripening figs, while Borges wonders *What became
of the century of light*? Thinking, this courtyard

a temple, his mother the watering hole of an eye
he can jump into and see, because faith is where
you drink from, between trust and vision.

Last Supper

If pain is the shadow of death
joy is the light we work toward.
The communion of us.

Love, an anesthesia.
Spilled blood, a lacquer.

We die, but we roll
stones from our caves—

listen to gospel
while godspell

blows
through our hair.

Portrait of Dylan Thomas

Wales   made of winter ·   coal.
Shale   dank and dark

but the day I climbed   to his boathouse   the sun
shone on the bay below   and the breakers   his poems.

My gaze entered through windows—to a desk of papers   a dry bottle.
His view of the limitless sea   where he would leave a wife and child
set sail   for America   dead at thirty-nine

with a ream of poems

read by those suffering

during a pandemic.

Portrait with *Francis Bacon,* Study for a Running Dog

From a distance, the dog runs
toward us, along railroad tracks
on a life-size canvas—

blurry, double exposure, time-lapse.
Half a second of film, quick enough
to trick the eye, an optical illusion.

A whisk, the dog is returning
from the adventure of late.
What smells, what find available.

The evening journey is an old bone,
carcass of a dead rat. A dog scurries
between rails still hot

from the sun and friction of the train,
his four legs one after another,
warming himself in winter light

on his way back home, if he has
a home. Running, because all
has been sniffed, sighted, and felt.

No more rabbits left to point and chase
or rough bark of trees to rub against.
And he is running, *maybe* home to a boy,

a family who will feed him
the guaranteed meal. A boy who will
save the beast delicious scraps of fat

then rub his freckled belly
while the animal's legs stand
suspended in air. Complete

and ordinary submissiveness.
But that is later. Just now, the dog
is panting, tired from the simple

brilliance of the new day, hungry
and longing for the companionship
of a boy who has come from Dublin,

who calls for him in his own name,
Fraaaancis! Child whose mind
wanders into an image of teeth

at the base of a crucifixion.
A boy who will love him
and never, not ever beat him.

To Basquiat at the Guggenheim

The ascending
spiral will lead us
to you—a crown,
head in heaven.

No stairs
in the building
or obstruction
in your vision.

Angels dressed
in turmeric tulle,
cobalt, cadmium,
bold as this planet.

This gleaming
white building
with you at its apex.
Symbol. Righteousness.
Like the young men
who replicate

your paintings
on the backs
of their jackets,
who guide me home
to my sister in Brooklyn.

Portraits in the National Gallery

In the green room   underlit

hangs a painting the size of a small mirror
where you have lost yourself.

In this room of the dead   heavy scent
of paint   no longer exists.

Inclusion

See how *author* is included in *authority*
and bleached bones of fish lie leached
on the beach in sun

A congregation of ravens rave on
our rooftop when we wake   sunlight
coming on   like a furnace   radiant

and the young savor song   sing
through their ring-studded tongues
pierced with halos   like saviors

Portrait of an Old Dog with Crooked Teeth

Faithful shadow, jigsaw
fence of crooked teeth.
All night bark. Protector.
Sheath.

Effigy with Horns

Little talisman, devil guardian.
Knives on head to ward off illness.

Effigy with Shell

Breathing spiral.

Oral female.

Sanctuary of cool

rose-colored tongue.

Medusa

If the snakes in your head return, force
people to fade, rooms to darken,

if you wake on the floor, as you have
dozens of times before, brain coiled,

tail rattled, tongue forked,

Medusa, having tasted the afterlife,
will you return to tell it?

Modern Colosseum

There is harmony in the weight machines
tone in these muscle men   straining
their deltoids   and the beautiful

abdominals cleaning up   as Joey works
on his buff   until it appears as if
he is polished stone   slick with sweat

while Billy of the silver-pierced nipples
flanked by tattooed arms of sharks
keeps working on an image of a saint

punctured with pain   a martyr   inked
with contrition   whereas Leon flexes
on the bench press in front of a flickering

TV   face thin and drawn from HIV
To remain fervent as gladiators
wrestling through an architecture

of perfect proportion   the men
become a sermon of the body
their physical address   a homily

On the Morning That Follows My Death

my teeth will be a forest for insects
while my son releases these pearls around my neck
as they weave and drip through his long, beautiful fingers.

Perhaps he will fasten them around someone who lives
in Seattle—or Delhi. Someone whose eyes stare at his
in a photograph he might carry in a black-stitched wallet.

In the morning after my death, one brother will order
an autopsy. One sister will stare at bare mesas, while
another asks for an open casket Rosary, but my organs

and bones will be loaned to someone in need of
an organ or bone. The empty sack of the body, burned.
Ashes to ashes. And my son will combine his father's
with mine. *Pax domini. Pax domini.*

Death of the Botanist

Having failed at all rituals,
paid the healer without a cure,

we wrapped her in a shroud, buried her
in the orchard, ripe with fruit, scent

of mint and fennel. This earth
she weeded. Wore leather gloves,

altered land where cattle
once drifted, unattended.

Terrain where she harvested stones
for walls, identified breakfast in a field.

Hum of elegy in the script of vine,
gnarled apple tree, shot-up gentian.

Our lament—evolving hymn—
leaves in wind, honeybee,

redwing blackbird to finch,
requiem swoop of a red-tailed hawk.

How we mystify from this atlas,
buried in sediment, an entire garden

flourishing above her.

Visions of Johanna, jpg #12

I listen to "Visions of Johanna"
while writing about you

when someone sends an email
containing a folder of photographs.

A picture of you at ten
with that crashed-in look.

I recall the narrative you recounted
when your grandmother swept you away

from the abuse, gave you a 0.22 rifle,
a pole, and a Buck knife, taught you

survival skills. What shocks me
is the final photo, jpg #12

which your first wife has taken
with her iPhone

only twenty-four hours before—
just as I had seen you on your deathbed.

So beautifully gaunt, it is like a picture
of the body crossing between worlds.

A wavering. One eye at half-mast,
a wet opening, viewing us instead.

Always looking ahead. A window
refusing to close.

I stored the picture in my memory.
Now, it sits on a bright screen in my house,

overlit, as if someone smuggled you out.
Your skin, yellow—the liver, I'm reminded.

They dressed you in your favorite green
shirt, buttoned up, crisp looking, tucked the wool

and cotton blankets around your body,
save for the long feet hanging over the bed,

which made me think of Jesus when the three Marys
held him after he was brought down from the cross.

No one knows the conversation
my son and I had over his father in that hour.

Do you want to lie down with him? *Yes.*
We held each weighted, cool hand, touched his hair.

He has taken care of his father for the last month,
slid drops of morphine down his throat, guarded

the door against unwelcome guests
like three-headed Cerberus.

We discussed his ears. I spoke of the left,
deformed by frostbite, told my son the tale—

fishing in a remote lake above the timberline,
snowstorm, struggled to get out.

He asked for more.
Once this body was taut as a rope,

disappeared nine meters through blue
water to hook spiny lobster.

We lived in Mexico.
Once, we traded fish for fruit.

All Souls

Under the gold of a Hunter's Moon,
I run into a large raccoon, ascending
an ancient piñon.

It's just like my mother
who died last week at ninety-six
to appear as this—clever, masked,
climbing with her small deft hands.

She loved creatures, the costumes
her children dressed in: one brood
of goblins, a vampire, the baby
sateened into a red-tailed devil.

My mother is here. I need to light fires—
torch yellow beeswax candles, sing
hymns to the moon, offer prayers.

I had never seen this mammal in the desert
but here she is, large-spirited, on a clear
evening, scaling October's end.

Time to remember auspicious numbers,
the faithful departed, our most revered
martyrs—this one, who carried me holy.

Prudent and ravenous for *this* world
I canonize her Demeter,
ghost, autumn spirit.

Dinner with Hades

It's my birthday, yet he sends *me* an invitation. I grow tired of his knock-knock jokes. *Knock, knock. Who's there? Hell. Hell who? Knock, knock. Who's there? Obsolete. Obsolete who?* And he goes into this lather of hysterical laughter, prepares a cake with mercury and Roman candles. His house, a collection of figures from ancient Greece, Asia Minor, Major, carvings of rich woods, mother-of-pearl, carpets of extinct animals, and rugs dyed with botanicals no longer in existence. From Mongolia, a red lacquer bed, made up with sheets of silvered fur. He serves everything foreign to my tongue. If I had known the delicate meat stuffed with heavy cream had been the body parts of fallen angels, I would not have eaten them. He devours his food voraciously; the thin bones of those lofty creatures slip from his glossy fingers.

I glance from the window through steel bars, note a hunting sleigh fashioned of cast iron, his vehicle for carnage. Above a table of marble hovers a candelabra of ivory tapers. The wax drips slick. He peers at me with pharmaceutical eyes, blue and amber. Closes them. Opens only one, like the hinged lid of a pot. Boiling steam. White mist. How cunning he is, as he rises, walks by the beveled mirror vacant of reflection.

He shows me a birthday cake, candled. My name is written in pomegranate seeds. It's like vertigo. Just before he seeks to devour, he halts to birdsong— sound of goldfinch, bluebird, hawk, lilting of sparrows. Of whippoorwill and dove. Wings flap, so many wings, a cool breeze as leaves unfurl into a once forgotten green and I am back on earth, held in my mother's arms.

At last, it is spring.

Born on Rembrandt's Birthday

It was July. The delivery, separating the selves
exhausted us all. Jars of paint emptied into our lives.
Jewel colors.

I had the taste for iron, soup of gold, and half tones.
Mica, pigment of red lake, lead white. Ultramarine
for the mother of Christ.

In the mirror, I caught a glimpse of him—Rembrandt.
Self-portraits. Broken blood vessels, the corner
of an eye, a lower lip glistening.

Deepened in mineral, ochre, shadowed in boneblack
char, and ash, soaked in his light.

Pandemia, Mouth of Insomnia

Something cave-like about the mouth
open while asleep, bats escaping with dreams.

Carlsbad Caverns with its broken teeth
of stalactites, stalagmites, sloshing

underwater in a Mediterranean grotto
or prayer mumbled before the Garden

of Gethsemane. Tonight I surrender
to breath. What I have. What I have left—

to the first home built on the side of a cliff
or wherever that last inhalation may take us.

If not in sleep, present with the thousand
daydreams of night.

Let worry go.

Politico

Because his poems draw blood
I am hooked. Did I tell you
he whispers sonnets at the edge
of annihilation? In a seduction?
Did I say time slows
when he enters a room?
On his forehead sits a tattoo
of a third eye with a lid. It opens.

To the Temple of Ghosts
he sends letters to my mother.
The man understands dialects
derived from out-of-body experience.
Did I mention the boy peers
through telescopes, discovers
future planets? I march in my dreams
to the Department of Incorruptibles,
ask for guidance from saints
and martyrs. For benedictions,
instructions.

My heart is on pause.
I won't let him steal it.

God of Nightfall

A neophyte
in the congregation
I could learn
from the queen
of bees and mothers
I'm done with walls called sacred
Give me a cathedral of stars
indigo sky with pearl spark
tumble of meteor shower
swift inaudible moments

I want constellations
of gods *and* goddesses
Madonna in cottonwood
fur and wing
Not some tired leader
or the Lord of Suffering

Sky   humble us
in our weariness
Fable the bleeding
Ghost the grief
Seek us forward
glancing back

Lend us celestial paradise
when earth undoes us
A sanctuary accessible
to the rich *and* the penniless
in this endless universe
full of mystery and science

blue moons

red giants   black holes

comets   .

asteroids   planets

Act of Faith

Plant one hyacinth
bulb above water.
One day a single green shoot
divides into two strapped leaves
as winter days gather
justice so close to the brink
you nearly reach out to caress it
the red flicker on the other side
of your window while days swim
by in dreams and duty
cooking beans, reading mail
alone in a world of lockdown
while one side of this purple flower
each day blooms into tiny florets
until its entire fist opens lilac,
and you, your house lifts
in fragrance. Remember the air
infused with pine following the deer
who appeared at the edge
of gold chanterelle. Your mother
in her honeysuckle. A son's
full laughter, building forts
in the arroyo behind juniper,
and beans on the stove frothing
like black rosary beads
while the flower crown
in the center of your house of god
fuses the air you breathe
with remembrance, and you
are hungry, and you eat.

NOTES

Page 3   A grand mal is an epileptic seizure causing an unconscious state in which the body becomes rigid.

Page 14   The quoted passage is a letter by Joan's mother, Isabelle, written in the mid-fifteenth century.

Page 17   Marie Curie is known for her discovery of the elements polonium and radium. Barred from advanced education in her native Poland, she moved to Paris in 1891 to study at the Sorbonne.

Page 22   The artist Caravaggio (1571–1610) painted in Rome. Mary died in Ephesus.

Page 33   A *castrato* (plural *castrati*) is a male singer with a voice similar to that of a soprano or mezzo-soprano. The voice was typically produced by castrating a boy singer before the onset of puberty. The practice was made illegal in the Papal States, the last to prohibit it, in 1870.

Page 38   In the poem *Rembrandt, Late Self-Portrait*, "boneblack" and "lead white" refer to two pigments often used by the painter.

Page 44   Francis Bacon (1909–1992) was a victim of child abuse. His large painting, *Study for a Running Dog*, is housed at the National Gallery of Art in Washington, DC.

ACKNOWLEDGMENTS

My thanks to the editors of the following journals in which these poems first appeared, sometimes in different form.

Canary: "Death of the Botanist"
Choice Words: "New Religion"
Diode: "Gods of a Grand Mal"
Fledging Rag: "Apnea," "Ars Poetica," "Our Lady of Broken Waters," and "Sometimes We Slip Out of Our Bodies"
Gargoyle: "Rembrandt, Late Self-Portrait" and "Visions of Johanna, jpg #12"
Hong Kong Review: "Intensive Care"
The Los Angeles Review: "Missing"
New Guard: "Dinner with Hades" republished in *Dime Stories*
Oranges & Sardines: "Born on Rembrandt's Birthday"
One: "Portrait of Marie Laveau"
Poetry Northwest: "To Basquiat at the Guggenheim"
Santa Fe Writers Project: "Portrait of Orpheus, Frida Kahlo, Love & Death"
Sin Fronteras/Writers without Borders: "Study of a Woman in the Woods"
Tahoma Literary Review: "All Souls"
The American Journal of Poetry: "Portrait of Caravaggio Painting *Death of the Virgin*," "Fentanyl," "On the Morning that Follows My Death," "Pandemia, Mouth of Insomnia," and "Politico"
Thrush: "Appointment with Dr. Siegel"

Much gratitude to Leila Chatti for selecting this manuscript as the Wheelbarrow Books Prize winner and to Anita Skeen and Gabe Dotto for guiding it into fruition.

I am grateful to Deborah Casillas and my husband, Ken Apt, for their thoughtful and insightful suggestions for this book.

Many thanks to Richard Lehnert for his astute editing.

Gratitude to Heather Derr, Frank Paino, and Lee Upton.

Great appreciation to the artist photographer, Daniella van Zadelhoff.

Gracias to my long-standing writing group: Tina Carlson, Deborah Casillas, Robyn Covelli-Hunt, Donald Levering, Anne Haven McDonnell, Gary Worth Moody, and Barbara Rockman.

Thanks to friends and writers Deanna Einspahr, Ginger Legato, Leslie Reynolds, Patti Reuss, Zoe Robles, Sarah Wolbach, and Jean Fogel Zee.

SERIES ACKNOWLEDGMENTS

We at Wheelbarrow Books have many people to thank without whom Mary Morris's *Late Self-Portraits* would never be in your hands. We begin by thanking all those writers who submitted manuscripts to the ninth Wheelbarrow Books Prize for Poetry. We want to single out the finalists: Jennifer Boydan, *We Can't Tell if the Constellations Love Us*; Marion Boyer, *The Ice Hours*; Jeff Knorr, *Fire Season*; and Lena Tuffaha, *Kaan and her Sisters* whose manuscripts moved and delighted us and which we passed on to the final judge, along with Mary Morris's manuscript, for her reading. That judge, Leila Chatti, we thank for her thoughtful selection of the winner and her critical comments offered earlier in this book.

Our thanks to Lauren Russell, Director of the RCAH Center for Poetry, for her support of Wheelbarrow Books, and Poetry Center interns, Jayla Harris-Hardy, Charlotte Krause, Kaylee McCarthy, and Fabrizzio Torero, for their careful reading of manuscripts and insightful commentary on their selections, and especially to Laurie Hollinger, assistant director at the RCAH Center for Poetry, who also read manuscripts and provided the logistical aid and financial wizardry for this project. Sarah Teppen, a previous RCAH Center for Poetry intern, designed our Wheelbarrow Books logo which makes us smile every time we see it.

We thank Stephen Esquith, dean of the Residential College in the Arts and Humanities, who has given his continued support to the RCAH Center for Poetry and Wheelbarrow Books since our inception. As we began thinking seriously about Wheelbarrow Books, conversation with June Youatt, then provost at Michigan State University, was encouraging, and MSU Press director Gabriel Dotto and former assistant director/editor-in-chief Julie Loehr were eager to support the efforts of poets to reach a hungry audience. We cannot thank them enough for having faith in us, and a love of literature, to collaborate on this project.

Thanks to our current editorial board, Sarah Bagby, Gabrielle Calvocoressi, Leila Chatti, Mark Doty, George Ellenbogen, Carolyn Forché, Thomas Lynch, George Ella Lyon, and Naomi Shihab Nye, for believing Wheelbarrow Books a worthy undertaking and lending their support and their time to our success.

Finally, to our patrons: without your belief in the Wheelbarrow Books Poetry Series and your generous financial backing, we would still be sitting around the conference table adding up our loose change. You are making it possible for poets who have never had a book of poetry published, something that's becoming harder and harder these days with so many presses discontinuing their publishing of poetry, to find an outlet for their work. You are also supporting the efforts of established poets to continue to reach a large and grateful audience. We name you here with great admiration and appreciation:

Beth Alexander   Mary Hayden
Gayle Davis   Patricia and Robert Miller
Fred Kraft   Brian Teppen
Jean Krueger

WHEELBARROW BOOKS

Anita Skeen, *Series Editor*

Sarah Bagby   Carolyn Forché
Mark Doty   Thomas Lynch
George Ellenbogen   Naomi Shihab Nye

Wheelbarrow Books, established in 2016, is an imprint of the RCAH Center for Poetry at Michigan State University, published and distributed by MSU Press. The biannual Wheelbarrow Books Poetry Prize is awarded every year to one emerging poet who has not yet published a first book and to one established poet.

SERIES EDITOR: Anita Skeen, professor in the Residential College in the Arts and Humanities (RCAH) at Michigan State University, founder and past director of the RCAH Center for Poetry, director of the Creative Arts Festival at Ghost Ranch, and director of the Fall Writing Festival

The RCAH Center for Poetry opened in the fall of 2007 to encourage the reading, writing, and discussion of poetry and to create an awareness of the place and power of poetry in our everyday lives. We think about this in a number of ways, including through readings, performances, community outreach, and workshops. We believe that poetry is and should be fun, accessible, and meaningful. We are building a poetry community in the Greater Lansing area and beyond. Our undertaking of the Wheelbarrow Books Poetry Series is one of the gestures we make to aid in connecting good writers and eager readers beyond our regional boundaries. Information about the RCAH Center for Poetry at MSU can be found at http://poetry.rcah.msu.edu and also at https://centerforpoetry.wordpress.com and on Facebook and Twitter (@CenterForPoetry).

The mission of the Residential College in the Arts and Humanities at Michigan State University is to weave together the passion, imagination, humor, and candor of the arts and humanities to promote individual well-being and the common good. Students, faculty, and community partners in the arts and humanities have the power to focus critical attention on the public issues we face and the opportunities we have to resolve them. The arts and humanities not only give us the pleasure of living in the moment but also the wisdom to make sound judgments and good choices.

The mission, then, is to see things as they are, to hear things as others may, to tell these stories as they should be told, and to contribute to the making of a better world. The Residential College in the Arts and Humanities is built on four cornerstones: world history, art and culture, ethics, and engaged learning. Together they define an open-minded public space within which students, faculty, staff, and community partners can explore today's common problems and create shared moral visions of the future. Discover more about the Residential College in the Arts and Humanities at Michigan State at http://rcah.msu.edu.